T0267048

THE ART OF CHARACTER ENTERTAINMENT LICENSING

A Guide to Licensing Success

CREATIVE CAPITAL PRESS

AHSAAN MITCHELL

ISBN 979-8-98862-192-8

CONTENTS

INTRODUCTION...1

WHAT IS CHARACTER ENTERTAINMENT LICENSING?.....3

HOW DOES CHARACTER ENTERTAINMENT
LICENSING WORK?...8

THE BENEFITS OF CHARACTER ENTERTAIMENT
LICENSING 16

KEY CONSIDERATIONS AND CHALLENGES
IN CHARACTER ENTERTAINMENT LICENSING 26

SUCCESSFUL EXAMPLES OF CHARACTER
ENTERTAINMENT LICENSING...................................31

TIPS FOR SUCCESS IN CHARACTER
ENTERTAINMENT LICENSING...................................36

GLOSSARY 68

THE ART OF CHARACTER
ENTERTAINMENT
LICENSING

INTRODUCTION

Character entertainment licensing promises to be an exhilarating ride, so get on board! This comprehensive guidebook will teach you everything you need to understand regarding character entertainment licensing for your favorite characters, as we dig into the inner workings of this rapidly growing industry.

From Mickey Mouse to Harry Potter, characters have been a cornerstone of popular culture for decades, capturing the hearts and imaginations of audiences around the world. But did you know that these beloved characters are also valuable commodities, with millions of dollars generated each year through licensing agreements? In fact, the global licensed merchandise market is expected to reach $392 billion by 2026, up from $280 billion in 2020.

So, whether you're a creator looking to monetize your characters, or a business looking to tap into the power of established brands, Character Entertainment Licensing is a lucrative and exciting opportunity that shouldn't't be ignored.

The purpose of this book is to explain what Character Entertainment Licensing is, how it operates, and the potential benefits it can offer to content producers and distributors. In addition, we'll discuss some of the most important factors to think about and obstacles to overcome when licensing characters, as well as offer advice on how to strike advantageous licensing deals.

So, buckle up and get ready to dive into the fascinating world of Character Entertainment Licensing!

CHAPTER 1:
WHAT IS CHARACTER ENTERTAINMENT LICENSING?

Character Entertainment Licensing is the process of authorizing the commercial use and reproduction of a character by a third party. Toys, apparel, video games, rides at amusement parks, and other things can now be based on these characters thanks to this licensing.

Typically, well-known characters with an existing fan base are chosen to be licensed. These icons typically enjoy high levels of name recognition and devoted fan bases. Comic novels, movies, and television shows are all potential sources. In order to capitalize on the desire for new products and experiences based on these popular characters, many companies have turned to licensing agreements with the rights holders.

New and original characters with a compelling concept or design can also be licensed by businesses. During the licensing process, it may be necessary to demonstrate the character's potential and make a strong commercial case to prospective licensees.

Character licensing may be very lucrative for creators. It's a great way for them to make money off their work even after it's been used in one media. Merchandise, video games, and other commercial products can feature a character that first appeared in a comic book series thanks to licensing.

In exchange for allowing others to use their creations, creators might get financial compensation in the form of royalties or licensing fees.

Brands and businesses alike can grow through licensing. Brands can expand their reach and increase sales by licensing popular characters. If an animated character is particularly well-liked, the rights holders may decide to license him or her for usage in theme park attractions. This benefits the character's owner and the licensee by increasing fan interaction and loyalty while also providing additional revenue opportunities.

In addition, the dangers of using unproven characters are lessened by licensing well-known ones. Companies have a better chance of selling plenty of licensed merchandise if they choose to collaborate with well-loved characters who already have an established fan base.

In a nutshell, "Character Entertainment Licensing" is a method by which companies can cash in on the fame and wealth associated with well-known characters. It gives artists a new method to make money and helps established companies reach more customers by capitalizing on their current fan bases and brand recognition to develop innovative, in-demand products and services.

THE HISTORY OF CHARACTER ENTERTAINMENT LICENSING

It all started with a mouse.

In the 1920s, Walt Disney was just a struggling animator who had a dream of inventing a new sort of entertainment. He eventually became the most successful person in the entertainment industry. He was already the creator of a few successful animated shorts, but he desired to work on a project of a greater scope. Something that would win the affections and spark the imaginations of people in every region of the planet.

After that, in 1928, he came up with the character Mickey Mouse.

Disney soon came to the realization that he was in possession of something truly remarkable when the endearing little rodent became an overnight phenomenon. He began selling licenses for the use of Mickey Mouse on a variety of products, and before long, the mouse was appearing on everything from toys to apparel to lunchboxes. Mickey Mouse was created by Walt Disney.

This marked the beginning of characters being licensed for use in entertainment.

Through the following few decades, Disney maintained its position as the industry leader in character licensing. They developed new characters such as Donald Duck, Goofy, and Snow White and then sold licensing rights to those characters to businesses in a variety of countries. By the 1950s, they had already reached a point where the licensing alone brought in millions of dollars annually.

Other businesses took note, and before long, the globe was teeming with characters who had licenses to operate. It appeared that there was no end to the characters that could be licensed, ranging from Superman to Barbie to Star Wars, and to the uses that those characters could have.

But with such tremendous achievement came enormous difficulties. It became increasingly difficult to differentiate oneself from the competition as an increasing number of businesses entered the character licensing market. In order to ensure that their characters remain current in the market, businesses needed to devise fresh and original uses for them.

The Teenage Mutant Ninja Turtles are regarded as one of the most effective examples of this phenomenon.

In the 1980s, a satirical take on the superhero genre was birthed in the form of the Ninja Turtles. However, they became an overnight sensation, and before long, they were the subject of licensing deals for a wide variety of products, including toys, video games, and even breakfast cereal.

However, the people who came up with the turtles were aware that they needed to do more if they wanted their characters to remain popular. As a result, they developed an animated television show that would go on to become one of the decade's most successful series.

The show put the turtles through a variety of crazy scenarios, and it played a role in maintaining the public's awareness of the characters for many years to come. Additionally, it was essential in the development of the concept of cross-media licensing, which outlined how characters may be adapted for use in a variety of types of media in order to appeal to a larger audience.

On the other hand, along with all this success came some drawbacks. It became increasingly difficult to safeguard the characters' original intentions as more and more businesses entered the character licensing market. Some businesses would either make unauthorized copies of well-known characters or use them in improper contexts, both of which would be detrimental to their reputations.

One of the most prominent illustrations of this phenomenon was the meteoric rise of the sector producing counterfeit Disney items in the 1990s. Companies in countries such as China and Thailand would produce low-quality knockoffs of well-known Disney characters and then sell those products in markets all over the world. Not only did this reduce Disney's income, but it also damaged the public's perception of the company's characters.

To prevent this, Disney has begun to crack down on items that is sold without a license and has begun to construct licensing agreements that are more stringent. They also started making significant investments in brand management, making sure that their characters were only utilized in ways that were positive for the firm and that the corporation was shown in a good light.

Companies from all around the world are competing with one another for a piece of the character entertainment licensing market, which is currently worth multiple billions of dollars. Nevertheless, despite the difficulties, it continues to be one of the most interesting and innovative areas of the entertainment industry.

Character licensing has been an important part of the development of our pop cultural landscape ever since the early days of Mickey Mouse and continues into the present era of superhero blockbuster movies. And there will always be a need for licensing in the entertainment sector so long as there are characters that catch our imaginations.

CHAPTER 2:

HOW DOES CHARACTER ENTERTAINMENT LICENSING WORK?

In most cases, the rights to use a character in a work of entertainment must be licensed from the character's creator or the company that acquired those rights (the business or individual seeking to use the character).

Licensors are responsible for managing and safeguarding the intellectual property connected with a particular character or brand, which makes them an essential component of the character licensing process. As a result, they play an important role in the licensing of characters. In this section, we will discuss the role of licensors in the licensing process and how they collaborate with creators and licensees to ensure that items bearing the brand's name are of a high quality and remain true to the brand's core principles.

First things first, let's talk about what exactly a licensor is. The owner of an item of intellectual property, such as a character, brand, or trademark, is referred to as the licensor of that item. It is the responsibility of the licensor to grant permission to third-party businesses or people, who are referred to as licensees, to make use of the intellectual property in exchange for a fee or a royalty.

The management of the licensing process is one of the most important responsibilities of a licensor, as is ensuring that licensed products have a high level of quality and are in line with the core values of the brand. In order to accomplish this goal, licensors generally devise licensing programs that detail the precise terms and conditions that licensees are expected to adhere to in order to maintain their rights. This program may include criteria for quality control and product safety, as well as recommendations on product design, packaging, and marketing. Additionally, this program may include guidelines on product design.

In addition, licensors play an essential part in the process of guarding their intellectual property from illegal use and acts of infringement. This may mean keeping an eye out on the market for products that aren't licensed, pursuing legal action against those who violate intellectual property rights, or collaborating with the authorities in charge of customs to stop the entry of fake goods.

Licensors have several vital roles, one of which is to collaborate with creators on the production of new intellectual property and the expansion of licensing programs. This may entail engaging with artists, writers, and other creators to produce new characters or brands, or it may mean expanding the licensing program into new product categories or markets. Both options are viable options.

Disney is a good example of a licensor that has been able to successfully manage its licensing program. Mickey Mouse, Marvel, and Star Wars are just a few of the well-known characters and brands that are owned by Disney, which makes the company one of the largest licensors in the entire globe. Disney has built a thorough licensing scheme that includes stringent restrictions on product design, packaging, and marketing as well as criteria for quality control and product safety. These guidelines and requirements may be found on Disney's website. This has been of assistance in ensuring that licensed products are of a high quality and keeping with the ideals associated with the brand.

Additionally, Disney collaborates intently with its licensees on the creation of new items and the expansion of the licensing program into new areas. For instance, Disney has just recently released a new range of toys and clothing based on the Marvel franchise, which was created in partnership with the Japanese shop Uniqlo. Because of this partnership, the licensing program was able to penetrate a previously untapped market and broaden its scope of potential customers.

In conclusion, licensors play an important part in the process of character licensing by managing and protecting intellectual property, ensuring that licensed products are of high quality and consistent with the brand's values, and working with creators and licensees to develop new intellectual property and expand the licensing program. In addition, licensors ensure that licensed products are of high quality and consistent with the brand's values. The ability of the licensor to effectively manage these diverse roles and to ensure that all parties involved are working towards the same goals is frequently a critical factor in determining whether a licensing program will be successful.

The licensing agreement spells out the specifics of the character's use, such as the types of goods and services that can be made, the geographical areas in which they can be sold, the length of time they can be used for, and the financial arrangements between the parties (such as royalties or upfront fees). The licensing agreement can specify quality control measures to be implemented on licensed products to guarantee they are up to par with the character's brand identity and consumer expectations. Character Entertainment Licensing Contracts Can Be One of Several Varieties, Such as:

AGREEMENTS FOR THE LICENSING OF CHARACTERS IN ENTERTAINMENT

Character entertainment licensing agreements are legally binding contracts that grant permission to a third party to exploit a character's name, image, and likeness for their own financial gain. These contracts can be divided down into numerous different sorts, each of which has its own set of distinguishing qualities and uses. In this article, we will examine the various types of character entertainment licensing agreements, such as those pertaining to merchandise, media, location-based entertainment, publishing, digital, music, sports, and food and beverage licensing. Specifically, we will focus on merchandise, media, and location-based entertainment.

LICENSES FOR THE SALE OF GOODS

Through the utilization of merchandise licensing agreements, third-party companies are granted permission to utilize the image and likeness of a character on things that they manufacture and sell. Toys, clothing, accessories, and even things to decorate your home could be among these offerings. In return for the permission to use the character, the licensee is required to pay the licensor a certain proportion of the profits made from the sale of products that bear the licensor's trademark.

Toy companies like Hasbro and Mattel, who produce and sell toys featuring characters from Disney movies and television episodes, get character licensing from The Walt Disney Company so that they can use such characters in their products.

MEDIA LICENSING

Under the terms of a media licensing deal, a character may be used by a third-party company in a variety of kinds of media, including films, television series, and video games. In return for the permission to use the character, the licensee is required to pay the licensor a percentage of the profits made by the media work that includes the licensed character.

Example: Marvel Entertainment grants movie studios like Sony and Disney permission to use their characters in their films. These studios then go on to produce and distribute films that star characters from the Marvel universe.

LICENSING FOR ENTERTAINMENT THAT IS BASED ON LOCATION

Through licensing agreements for location-based entertainment, third-party companies are granted permission to utilize a character in a variety of themed attractions, including theme parks, museums, and live shows. In order to obtain permission to use the character, the licensee is required to pay the licensor a certain proportion of the profits made by the location-based entertainment that features the character that has been licensed.

For illustration, Universal Studios obtains permissions to use characters from the Harry Potter series in order to develop themed attractions such as "The Wizarding World of Harry Potter."

OBTAINING PERMISSION TO PUBLISH

Through the utilization of publishing license agreements, third-party companies are granted permission to utilize a character in printed materials such as books, comics, and other publications. The licensee is required to make a payment to the licensor in the form of a percentage of the profits made from the sale of licensed publications before they are granted permission to use the character.

As an illustration, DC Comics grants rights for the use of its characters to other comic book publishers, such as Marvel Comics and Image Comics, so that those companies can make and market comic books that feature DC characters.

DIGITAL LICENSING

Through the utilization of digital licensing agreements, third-party companies are granted permission to use a character in various forms of digital media, including websites, mobile apps, and video games. In return for the permission to use the character, the licensee agrees to pay the licensor a certain percentage of the profits made by the digital material that features the licensed character.

THE CRAFT OF LICENSING CHARACTERS FOR ENTERTAINMENT PURPOSES

For illustration purposes, Rovio Entertainment offers the characters from its Angry Birds franchise for licensing in order to facilitate the development of mobile applications and video games utilizing the well-known birds.

LICENSING OF MUSICAL WORKS

Music licensing agreements make it possible for third-party organizations to utilize the image and likeness of a character in connection with music-related products and services like albums, concerts, and music videos. These types of products and services include concerts and music videos. The licensee owes the licensor a certain percentage of the profits made from the music-related content that features the licensed character as payment for the right to use the character.

Example: The band's firm, Apple Corps, sells licenses to music streaming services like Spotify and Apple Music, as well as to businesses that manufacture items like t-shirts and posters, so that those businesses can use the band's image and likeness in their products.

LICENSES FOR SPORTING EVENTS

Under the terms of a sports licensing deal, third-party businesses are granted permission to use a character's name, image, and likeness in connection with the sale of sports-related goods and services such as apparel, video games, and sporting equipment. In return for the permission to use the character, the licensee is obligated to pay the licensor a certain proportion of the profits made from the sale of sports-related content that features the licensed character.

The National Football League, for instance, grants a license to video game developers such as EA Sports to use their teams and players in the football video games that they produce and sell. These games feature NFL clubs and players.

OBTAINING PERMISSION TO SERVE FOOD AND DRINK

The image and resemblance of a character can be used by a third-party company if a licensing agreement is in place for the food and beverage industry,

like with many consumable food and drink goods, including sweets, beverages, and snacks. In return for the permission to use the character, the licensee is required to make a payment to the licensor in the form of a percentage of the profits made from the sale of food and drink products that include the licensed character.

The Coca-Cola Company, known for its classic Christmas advertisements starring Santa Claus, has a license to use Santa Claus to promote holiday-themed beverages. This license allows Coca-Cola to promote its products using Santa Claus.

In conclusion, character entertainment licensing agreements are an essential component of the entertainment industry. These agreements grant businesses the right to use well-known characters in the production of a diverse variety of goods and services. Licensors and licensees can develop mutually beneficial collaborations that contribute to the generation of revenue and the promotion of their brands if they have an awareness of the many types of character entertainment licensing agreements

CHAPTER 3:

THE BENEFITS OF CHARACTER ENTERTAIMENT LICENSING

For creators, licensing their characters can provide a valuable revenue stream, allowing them to monetize their creations beyond their initial use in a specific medium. This can be particularly beneficial for independent creators, who may not have the resources to create and market their own merchandise or experiences.

ESTABLISHED BRAND RECOGNITION

One of the biggest advantages of licensing established characters is the pre-existing brand recognition they bring. Characters such as Mickey Mouse, Batman, and Spider-Man are instantly recognizable to millions of people around the world, making them highly marketable and appealing to consumers.

By leveraging the brand recognition of a well-known character, businesses can create products and experiences that are more likely to capture the attention of consumers and generate interest. This can result in increased sales, improved brand awareness, and a competitive advantage over other companies that don't have the same level of brand recognition.

ACCESS TO ESTABLISHED FAN BASES

In addition to brand recognition, licensing established characters can also provide businesses with access to a pre-existing fan base. Characters from popular franchises such as Star Wars, Harry Potter, and Marvel have dedicated fan communities that are passionate about the characters and their stories.

By licensing these characters, businesses can tap into these fan bases and create products and experiences that appeal to their interests and passions. This can help to build a strong following for the business, generate word-of-mouth marketing, and create a loyal customer base.

COST-EFFECTIVE MARKETING

Licensing established characters can also be a cost-effective way to market products and services. Because the characters already have a high level of brand recognition, businesses can use them to promote their products without having to spend as much on advertising and marketing campaigns

For example, a business that licenses a popular character for a product line can use the character's image and likeness in their marketing materials, creating a powerful visual association with the product. This can be more effective than spending money on traditional marketing campaigns that may not have the same level of impact.

INCREASED PRODUCT SALES

Another benefit of licensing established characters is the potential for increased product sales. Characters that are well-known and loved by consumers can help to drive sales by making products more appealing and desirable.

For example, a children's clothing company that licenses a popular character for a line of t-shirts may see increased sales as a result of the character's popularity and appeal to children. Similarly, a video game company that licenses a popular character for a new game may see increased sales as a result of the character's fan base and appeal to gamers.

EXPANDED PRODUCT LINES

Licensing established characters can also provide businesses with opportunities to expand their product lines. By licensing a popular character, businesses can create new products and experiences that leverage the character's existing fan base and appeal.

For example, a toy company that licenses a popular character may be able to create a range of different toys and games based on the character, such as action figures, board games, and puzzles. Similarly, a theme park that licenses a popular character may be able to create new rides and attractions based on the character's stories and adventures.

COLLABORATION OPPORTUNITIES

Finally, licensing established characters can provide businesses with opportunities for collaboration and partnership. By partnering with the owners of popular characters, businesses can create co-branded products and experiences that appeal to a wider audience.

For example, a clothing company that licenses a popular character may be able to collaborate with a shoe company to create a line of co-branded shoes featuring the character's image and likeness. Similarly, a video game company that licenses a popular character may be able to partner with a movie studio to create a co-branded movie based on the character's story.

REDUCED RISK AND COST

Creating a new character or brand from scratch can be a risky and expensive endeavor. It requires significant investment in design, development, and marketing, with no guarantee of success. Licensing an established character can help to reduce some of these risks and costs.

DESIGN AND DEVELOPMENT COSTS

Design and development costs in character licensing can be substantial, as they involve various stages and specialized skills. Here's a detailed breakdown of the design and development process, along with examples to illustrate each step:

1.CHARACTER CONCEPTUALIZATION:

Brainstorming: This initial stage involves generating ideas for the character's appearance, personality, and backstory. For instance, the team behind "Pokémon" brainstormed various creatures with unique abilities, resulting in characters like Pikachu and Charizard.

Market Research understanding the target audience's preferences and trends helps shape the character's design. The creators of "My Little Pony" conducted market research to develop characters that appealed to young girls, leading to the creation of Twilight Sparkle, Rainbow Dash, and others.

2. CHARACTER DESIGN:

Sketches and Concepts: Artists create rough sketches and concept art to visualize the character's appearance, including details like facial features, costumes, and accessories. The development of characters like "Spider-Man" involved multiple iterations of costume designs before settling on the iconic red and blue suit.

Iterative Process: Designers refine the character's visual elements based on feedback and internal reviews. Pixar's development of characters like Woody and Buzz Lightyear in "Toy Story" went through numerous iterations to achieve the perfect balance of appeal and believability.

3. ARTISTIC DEVELOPMENT:

Model Sheets: Detailed model sheets are created, providing reference points for consistency in the character's pro-portions, poses, and expressions. The character "Mickey Mouse" has a well-defined model sheet that ensures his iconic appearance remains consistent across different media and merchandise.

Color Design: Colorists determine the character's color palette, considering factors like brand identity and visual appeal. Characters like "SpongeBob SquarePants" have dis-tinct color schemes that contribute to their recognizability and marketability.

4. STORY AND PERSONALITY DEVELOPMENT:

compelling backstory and personality traits for the character. The character "Wonder Woman" was conceptualized as an Amazonian princess with a strong sense of justice and a desire to protect the innocent.

Character Arcs: Writers explore the character's growth and development throughout their storylines, ensuring consistency and evolution. Characters like "Iron Man" undergo character arcs that transition from self-centered playboy to selfless hero.

5. TECHNICAL DEVELOPMENT:

3D Modeling: In the case of digital media or merchandise requiring 3D representation, artists and modelers create digital models of the character. The character "Elsa" from Disney's "Frozen" underwent intricate 3D modeling to capture her intricate ice dress and magical abilities.

Animation and Rigging: Animators bring the character to life by creating movement and expressions. Pixar's characters, such as "Woody" and "Buzz Lightyear," require complex rigging systems to achieve their unique movements and facial expressions.

6. MARKET TESTING AND REFINEMENT:

Consumer Feedback: Testing the character's appeal through focus groups or surveys helps identify areas for improvement. The development of characters like "Superman" involved gathering feedback from comic book readers to refine his abilities and persona.

Iterative Refinement: Feedback is incorporated into the character's design and development process, resulting in continuous refinement to ensure market acceptance and longevity.

By licensing an established character, businesses can skip the entire design and development process outlined above. Instead, they can leverage the character's existing design, fan base, and market appeal, reducing time and costs associated with creating a new character from scratch.

MARKETING COSTS:

Marketing a new character or brand can also be a significant expense. It requires creating awareness of the character among potential customers and convincing them to buy products or services associated with the character.

Licensing an established character can help to reduce some of these marketing costs. The character already has a built-in fan base and market appeal, which can help to generate interest and sales without the need for extensive marketing campaigns. For example, a company that licenses the Harry Potter brand for a line of products can leverage the existing fan base to promote the products, rather than having to create a new marketing campaign from scratch.

EXAMPLES:

1.MARVEL COMICS:

Marvel Comics is a great example of how licensing established characters can be beneficial for businesses. The company has created a vast universe of characters, including Spider-Man, Iron Man, and the Avengers, that have become incredibly popular among fans of all ages. By licensing these characters to other companies, Marvel has been able to generate significant revenue and expand its reach beyond the world of comics.

For example, Marvel has licensed the Spider-Man character to Sony Pictures for use in movies, resulting in a series of highly successful films that have grossed billions of dollars at the box office. Marvel has also licensed its characters to video game companies, resulting in popular games like Spider-Man: Miles Morales and Marvel's Avenger

2. DISNEY:

Disney is another great example of how licensing established characters can be beneficial for businesses. The company has created some of the most iconic characters in history, including Mickey Mouse, Cinderella, and Buzz Lightyear. By licensing these characters to other companies, Disney has been able to generate significant revenue and expand its reach beyond its core businesses of movies and theme parks.

For example, Disney has licensed its characters to toy companies like Hasbro and Mattel, resulting in popular toys and games that have generated millions of dollars in sales. Disney has also licensed its characters to clothing companies like H&M and Gap, resulting in popular clothing lines for children and adults.

3. STAR WARS:

The Star Wars franchise is a great example of how licensing established characters can help to revive a brand that has gone dormant. After the release of the original Star Wars trilogy in the 1970s and 1980s, the franchise went quiet for several years. However, when the prequel trilogy was released in the late 1990s and early 2000s, the franchise was reignited and has since become one of the most popular franchises in history.

By licensing the Star Wars brand to other companies, Lucasfilm (the company behind the franchise) has been able to generate significant revenue and expand the reach of the franchise. For example, the company has licensed the Star Wars brand to toy companies like LEGO and Hasbro, resulting in popular toys and games that have generated millions of dollars in sales. Lucasfilm has also licensed the Star Wars brand to clothing companies like Uniqlo and Levi's, resulting in popular clothing lines for fans of all ages

4. POKÉMON:

Pokémon is another great example of how licensing established characters can be beneficial for businesses. The franchise started as a series of video games in the 1990s, but has since expanded to include trading cards, toys, movies, and more.

By licensing the Pokémon brand to other companies, The Pokémon Company (the company behind the franchise) has been able to generate significant revenue and expand the reach of the franchise. For example, the company has licensed the Pokémon brand to toy companies like TOMY and Jazwares, resulting in popular toys and games that have generated millions of dollars in sales. The Pokémon Company has also licensed the brand to clothing companies like H&M and Uniqlo, resulting in popular clothing lines for children and adults.

5. HELLO KITTY:

Hello Kitty is a Japanese character that has become a global phenomenon. The character is a white cat with a red bow and has been licensed for use on a wide variety of products, including clothing, toys, and home decor.

By licensing the Hello Kitty brand to other companies, San-rio (the company behind the character) has been able to gen-erate significant revenue and expand the reach of the brand. For example, Sanrio has licensed the Hello Kitty brand to toy companies like Mattel and Bandai, resulting in popular toys and games that have generated millions of dollars in sales.

Sanrio has also licensed the brand to clothing companies like Forever 21 and Converse, resulting in popular clothing lines for children and adults.

CONCLUSION

In conclusion, licensing established characters can provide several benefits for businesses, including reduced risk and cost, established brand recognition, and access to a pre-existing fan base and market appeal. The examples above demonstrate how licensing established characters can be used to generate significant revenue and expand the reach of a brand. By leveraging the popularity and appeal of an established character, businesses can create products and experiences that are more likely to capture the attention of consumers and generate interest, ultimately leading to increased sales and improved brand awareness.

OPPORTUNITIES FOR INNOVATION AND CREATIVITY

While licensing an established character may seem limiting in terms of creativity, it can provide opportunities for innovation and new ideas. By working within the framework of an established character, businesses can explore new and creative ways to use the character's brand and identity, while still maintaining its core characteristics and appeal.

For example, a clothing company that licenses a popular character may explore new and innovative designs that appeal to a wider range of consumers, while still staying true to the character's brand identity.

CHAPTER 4:

KEY CONSIDERATIONS AND CHALLENGES IN CHARACTER ENTERTAINMENT LICENSING

While Character Entertainment Licensing can be a lucrative and exciting opportunity, it's important to be aware of some of the key considerations and challenges involved in the process.

LICENSING FEES AND ROYALTIES

One of the biggest considerations in Character Entertainment Licensing is the financial arrangement between the licensor and licensee. Licensing fees and royalties can vary widely depending on the popularity and perceived value of the character, as well as the scope and duration of the licensing agreement.

For licensors, it's important to ensure that they are receiving fair compensation for the use of their character, while also considering the potential benefits to their brand and the exposure that licensing can provide.

For licensees, it's important to carefully consider the financial implications of a licensing agreement, including the cost of production, marketing, and distribution, as well as the potential return on investment.

QUALITY CONTROL

Another important consideration in Character Entertainment Licensing is quality control. Licensors need to ensure that the licensed products and experiences are consistent with the character's brand identity and meet certain standards of quality.

This can be challenging, particularly for licensees who may have different design or production standards than the li-censor. It's important for both parties to work closely together to establish clear guidelines and expectations for quality control.

COMPETITION AND MARKET SATURATION

Another challenge in Character Entertainment Licensing is competition and market saturation. With so many characters and properties available for licensing, it can be difficult for new or lesser-known characters to stand out and compete with established brands.

It's important for licensors and licensees to carefully consider the market demand for a particular character, as well as the level.

of competition in the market, before entering into a licensing agreement. This can help ensure that the licensed products and experiences have a better chance of success in a crowded marketplace.

MAINTAINING BRAND CONSISTENCY:

Maintaining brand consistency is another important consideration in Character Entertainment Licensing. Licensors need to ensure that the licensed products and experiences are consistent with the character's brand identity and values, in order to maintain the character's appeal to its fan base.

This can be challenging, particularly if a licensee has different ideas or creative approaches than the licensor. It's important for both parties to work closely together to ensure that the licensed products and experiences stay true to the character's brand identity and values.

BRAND IDENTITY AND VALUES:

The first step in maintaining brand consistency is to establish a clear brand identity and set of values for the character. This includes things like the character's personality traits, backstory, visual design, and core themes or messages.

Licensors need to ensure that the licensed products and experiences align with this brand identity and values, in order to maintain the character's appeal and credibility with its fan base. For example, a licensed product that portrays a typically heroic character as a villain might not be well received by fans and could damage the character's overall brand.

BRAND GUIDE LINES:

One way that licensors maintain brand consistency is by providing brand guidelines to licensees. These guidelines typically include instructions on how to use the character's likeness and visual design, as well as guidelines on tone, messaging, and other brand elements.

By providing clear guidelines, licensors can ensure that licensees are creating products and experiences that align with the character's brand identity and values, and that are consistent with the overall look and feel of the character's world.

QUALITY CONTROL:

Another important aspect of maintaining brand consistency is quality control. Licensors need to ensure that licensed products and experiences meet a certain level of quality and standards, in order to protect the character's brand reputation.

This can include things like ensuring that products are made from high-quality materials, that designs are accurate and true to the character's appearance, and that experiences meet certain safety and quality standards.

COLLABORATION WITH LICENSEES:

Finally, maintaining brand consistency requires collaboration between licensors and licensees. Licensors need to work closely with licensees to ensure that licensed products and experiences align with the character's brand identity and values, and that they meet certain quality standards.

This can involve providing feedback on product designs, re-viewing marketing materials, and collaborating on new product ideas and experiences.

EXAMPLES:

One example of a licensor that takes brand consistency seriously is The Walt Disney Company. Disney has a detailed set of brand guidelines that apply to all licensed products and experiences, ensuring that they align with the company's overall brand identity and values.

The Warner Bros. Entertainment-licensed Harry Potter se-ries is another example. The franchise has strict guidelines for licensed products, including guidelines on how to use the Harry Potter logo, how to depict the characters, and how to handle sensitive topics like magic and witchcraft.

CONCLUSION

In conclusion, maintaining brand consistency is an important consideration in Character Entertainment Licensing. By establishing a clear brand identity and set of values, providing brand guidelines, ensuring quality control, and collaborating with licensees, licensors can ensure that licensed products and experiences align with the character's brand and maintain its appeal to its fan base.

The examples above demonstrate how licensors like Disney and Warner Bros. enforce brand consistency in their licensed products and experiences, ultimately leading to increased brand recognition and market appeal.

CHAPTER 5:

SUCCESSFUL EXAMPLES OF CHARACTER ENTERTAINMENT LICENSING

While there are many successful examples of Character Entertainment Licensing, here are a few notable examples that showcase the benefits and opportunities of licensing established characters.

STAR WARS

George Lucas created the epic space opera series Star Wars in 1977. The franchise includes movies, TV shows, books, comic books, video games, and a wide range of merchandise.

Star Wars is one of the most successful entertainments franchises of all time, with a global box office revenue of over $10 billion and a dedicated fan base that spans all ages. The franchise's success can be attributed to its compelling characters, memorable storylines, and iconic designs.

Star Wars has been licensed for a wide range of products, including toys, clothing, home decor, and food and beverage products. One of the most successful examples of Star Wars licensing is the Star Wars: The Black

Series action figures, which are highly detailed and collectible figures that are popular among fans and collectors.

In addition to merchandise licensing, the Star Wars franchise has also been featured in several successful video games, including Star Wars Battlefront and Star Wars Jedi: Fallen Order. The franchise has also inspired several movies and TV shows.

HARRY POTTER

The Harry Potter franchise is another successful example of character entertainment licensing. Since the release of the first book in 1997, the franchise has expanded to include a wide range of products and experiences, including films, theme park attractions, and merchandise.

One of the keys to the franchise's success has been its ability to create a rich and immersive world that fans are passion-ate about. This has allowed licensees to create a wide range of products and experiences that appeal to different audiences, while staying true to the franchise's core themes and values.

POKÉMON

Pokémon is a Japanese media franchise created in 1995 that features fictional creatures called "Pokémon". The franchise includes video games, trading card games, an animated TV series, movies, and a wide range of merchandise.

Pokémon is one of the most successful entertainment franchises of all time, with over 25 billion cards sold and more than 340 million video games sold worldwide. The franchise's success can be attributed to its ability to appeal to a wide range of demographics, from young children to adults.

The Pokémon franchise has been licensed for a wide range of products, including toys, clothing, home decor, and food and beverage products. One of the most successful examples of Pokémon licensing is the Pokémon Trading Card Game, which has been a popular collectible card game since its introduction in 1996.

In addition to merchandise licensing, the Pokémon franchise has also been featured in several successful video games, including Pokémon Red and Blue, Pokémon Go, and Pokémon Sword and Shield. The franchise has also inspired several movies and a popular animated TV series.

The success of Pokémon licensing can be attributed to the franchise's strong brand identity and the appeal of the Pokémon characters. The colorful and cute designs of the Pokémon creatures have made them instantly recognizable and highly marketable, while the franchise's strong focus on collectability has created a dedicated fan base that is eager to collect all things Pokémon.

SPONGEBOB SQUAREPANTS

SpongeBob SquarePants is a beloved animated character who has become a cultural icon. The character was created by marine biologist and animator Stephen Hillenburg and made his debut on Nickelodeon in 1999. Since then, SpongeBob has become one of the most popular and recognizable characters in the world, with a fan base that spans all ages.

One of the most successful examples of SpongeBob licensing is the annual SpongeBob SquarePants Christmas Special, which features a line of holiday-themed products such as ornaments, pajamas, and stockings.

In addition to merchandise licensing, SpongeBob has also been featured in several successful video games, including SpongeBob SquarePants: Battle for Bikini Bottom and SpongeBob SquarePants: The Movie. The character has also been the inspiration for several theme park attractions, including

SpongeBob SquarePants 4-D: The Great Jelly Rescue and SpongeBob SquarePants Rock Bottom Plunge.

The success of SpongeBob SquarePants licensing can be attributed to the character's universal appeal and relatable personality. SpongeBob's humor and positive attitude make him a favorite among children and adults alike, and his adventures in Bikini Bottom provide a wealth of creative opportunities for licensees.

FAT ALBERT AND THE COSBY KIDS

"Fat Albert and the Cosby Kids" was a groundbreaking animated TV series that aired from 1972 to 1985. The program reflected Bill Cosby's own experiences growing up in Philadelphia. The series followed a group of African American kids, including the titular character Fat Albert, as they navigated the challenges and adventures of everyday life in their neighborhood.

One of the key themes of the show was education, with each episode featuring a moral lesson or message. The show was also notable for its positive representation of African American culture and community, and for promoting themes of friendship, teamwork, and self-esteem.

Despite the controversy surrounding Bill Cosby in recent years, "Fat Albert and the Cosby Kids" remains an important piece of African American television history. Here are some of the factors that contributed to the show's success:

POSITIVE REPRESENTATION

"Fat Albert and the Cosby Kids" was one of the first animated series to feature a predominantly African American cast. The show presented a positive representation of African American culture and community, and helped to counter the negative stereotypes that were prevalent in mainstream media at the time.

EDUCATIONAL CONTENT

Each episode of the show included a moral lesson or message, often focused on issues such as bullying, drug abuse, or peer pressure. The show was praised for its educational content, which helped to engage and inspire young viewers.

MEMORABLE CHARACTERS

The show featured a diverse cast of memorable characters, each with their own distinct personalities and quirks. The titular character Fat Albert, with his trademark catchphrase "Hey hey hey!", became an iconic figure in popular culture.

CREATIVE TEAM

The creative team behind "Fat Albert and the Cosby Kids" included some of the most talented animators and writers in the industry. The show's distinctive visual style and engaging storytelling helped to set it apart from other animated series of the time.

ENDURING LEGACY

Despite the controversy surrounding Bill Cosby, "Fat Albert and the Cosby Kids" remains a beloved piece of African American television history. The show has inspired numerous spin-offs, adaptations, and merchandise, and continues to resonate with audiences of all ages.

In conclusion, "Fat Albert and the Cosby Kids" was a ground-breaking animated TV series that had a significant impact on African American television history. The show's positive representation, educational content, memorable characters, and creative team helped to make it a success, and its enduring legacy continues to inspire and entertain audiences to this day

CHAPTER 6:

TIPS FOR SUCCESS IN CHARACTER ENTERTAINMENT LICENSING

If you're interested in pursuing Character Entertainment Licensing, here are a few tips to help you succeed in the industry.

DO YOUR RESEARCH

Before entering into a licensing agreement, it's important to do your research and understand the market demand for the character, as well as the level of competition in the market. This can help you make informed decisions about the potential success of licensed products and experiences.

ESTABLISH CLEAR GUIDELINES

It's important to establish clear guidelines and expectations for quality control, brand consistency, and other important considerations in a licensing agreement. This can help ensure that both parties are on the same page and can avoid potential disputes or issues down the line.

BE CREATIVE

While it's important to maintain brand consistency, there is still plenty of room for creativity and innovation within the framework of an established character. Look for opportunities to explore new and unique ways to use the character's brand and identity, while still staying true to its core characteristics and appeal.

IDENTIFY AND TARGET THE RIGHT AUDIENCE:

Understand the target demographic for your character and tailor your licensing strategy accordingly. Consider factors such as age group, interests, and consumer preferences to ensure your licensed products and experiences resonate with the intended audience.

BUILD A STRONG BRAND IDENTITY:

Develop a cohesive and recognizable brand identity for your character that sets it apart from competitors.

This includes creating a distinctive visual design, memorable catchphrases, and a compelling backstory that connects with fans.

COLLABORATE WITH REPUTABLE PARTNERS:

Seek out reputable licensees, partners, and distributors who align with your brand values and have a track record of success in the industry. Collaborating with established companies can help expand your reach and ensure high-quality products and experiences.

PROTECT YOUR INTELLECTUAL PROPERTY:

Prioritize the protection of your character's intellectual property through trademarks, copyrights, and other legal measures. Regularly monitor and enforce your rights to prevent unauthorized use and maintain control over your brand.

Embrace digital channels and social media platforms to engage with fans, build a community, and promote your licensed products and experiences. Utilize targeted advertising, influencer partnerships, and engaging content to increase brand visibility and connect with your audience.

CONTINUOUSLY INNOVATE AND ADAPT:

Stay attuned to market trends and consumer preferences. Regularly update and refresh your character's content, merchandise, and experiences to stay relevant and capture new opportunities in the ever-evolving entertainment landscape.

SEEK PROFESSIONAL GUIDANCE WHEN NEEDED:

Consider consulting with licensing experts, attorneys specializing in intellectual property law, and other professionals who can provide guidance and expertise throughout the licensing process. Their insights can help you navigate complex legal and business considerations effectively.

Remember, success in character entertainment licensing requires a combination of creativity, business acumen, and strategic decision-making.

By following these tips and remaining dedicated to your vision, you can increase your chances of building a successful and profitable character licensing venture.

FOCUS ON THE FAN BASE

Finally, it's important to focus on the character's fan base and their interests and preferences when developing licensed products and experiences. By understanding what the fans want and expect, you can create products and experiences that are more likely to capture their attention and generate interest.

CONCLUSION

Character Entertainment Licensing is a dynamic and exciting industry that offers many opportunities for businesses and entrepreneurs.

In the words of an industry expert, "Character entertainment licensing offers a world of opportunities for creators and businesses alike. Understanding the costs involved and navigating the various aspects of development, protection, and promotion is crucial for success in this dynamic industry."

As a bonus, here are a few additional pieces of information that may be useful for those interested in Character Entertainment Licensing.

THE ROLE OF SOCIAL MEDIA IN CHARACTER ENTERTAINMENT LICENSING.

Social media plays a crucial role in promoting and marketing licensed products and experiences in the realm of character entertainment licensing. Here are a few ways in which social media can be utilized:

BUILDING BUZZ AND EXCITEMENT

Social media platforms, such as Facebook, Instagram, Twitter, and YouTube, offer a direct and immediate way to engage with fans and build anticipation for new licensed products and experiences.

Example: Prior to the release of a new movie featuring a licensed character, the movie studio can use social media to share behind-the-scenes footage, trailers, and teasers, creating excitement and generating buzz among fans. This strategy was effectively employed by Marvel Studios in their promotion of Avengers: Endgame, with teaser posters and exclusive clips shared on social media platforms.

DIRECT FAN ENGAGEMENT AND FEEDBACK

Social media platforms provide a space for licensors and licensees to directly interact with fans, gaining insights and feedback on their licensed products and experiences

Example: Through social media, a video game company that licenses a popular character can actively engage with players, responding to their comments and suggestions, and even running polls or contests to involve the fan base in decision-making processes. This approach was seen with the release of the game Spider-Man: Miles Morales, where the developer, Insomniac Games, regularly engaged with fans on social media, addressing their questions and incorporating their feedback into the game.

USER-GENERATED CONTENT AND INFLUENCER MARKETING

Social media platforms allow fans to create and share their own content featuring licensed characters, providing valuable user-generated content that can further promote and amplify the reach of licensed products and experiences.

Example: Fans dressing up as their favorite licensed characters and sharing their cosplay photos on social media platforms not only generate buzz but also serve as a form of free advertising for licensed products. Additionally, influencer marketing can be leveraged, where popular social media influencers collaborate with licensors and licensees to promote licensed products to their large follower base. This tactic has been effectively utilized in the beauty industry, with influencers partnering with cosmetic brands to showcase licensed character-themed makeup collections.

COMMUNITY-BUILDING AND FAN COMMUNITIES

Social media platforms provide a space for fans to connect with each other, forming dedicated fan communities centered around licensed characters.

Example: Online fan groups or forums on social media platforms dedicated to specific licensed characters allow fans to share their love for the characters, discuss related content, and exchange recommendations for licensed products. These communities can foster a sense of belonging and create a dedicated customer base for licensed merchandise. For instance, the Harry Potter fan community has numerous Facebook groups where fans can share their experiences, interact with fellow fans, and discuss various licensed products.

The visibility, reach, and success of licensed products and experiences in the character entertainment industry can be greatly increased through the strategic use of social media by both licensors and licensees to generate excitement, engage directly with fans, leverage user-generated content, and foster thriving fan communities. Why Quality Assurance Is So Crucial Any poorly conceived or executed Character Entertainment Licensing product or experience can be detrimental to the character's name and popularity. All licensed products and experiences must be of the highest quality and consistency, and this requires close collaboration between the licensor and the licensee.

THE RISE OF EXPERIENTIAL LICENSING IN CHARACTER ENTERTAINMENT

Experiential licensing has become increasingly popular in the realm of character entertainment, offering fans immersive and interactive experiences that go beyond traditional merchandise. Here are some key points and examples:

IMMERSIVE THEME PARK ATTRACTIONS

Theme parks have embraced experiential licensing by cre-ating immersive attractions based on popular characters. These attractions transport visitors into the world of the character, allowing them to interact with the story and settings firsthand (Choi et al., 2019).

Example: The Wizarding World of Harry Potter at Universal Orlando Resort and Universal Studios Hollywood offers visitors the opportunity to explore iconic locations from the Harry Potter series, such as Hogwarts Castle and Diagon Alley. Guests can experience themed rides, sample wizarding treats, and even cast spells with interactive wands, immersing themselves in the magical world (Universal Parks & Resorts, n.d.).

LIVE SHOWS AND PERFORMANCES

Experiential licensing extends to live shows and performances, where fans can witness their favorite characters come to life on stage. These productions often incorporate music, dance, and interactive elements to engage the audience.

Example: Disney on Ice presents touring ice shows that bring beloved Disney characters, such as Mickey Mouse, Elsa, and Woody, to the stage. These productions combine ice skating, dazzling costumes, and storytelling to create a magical experience for families and fans of all ages.

INTERACTIVE EXHIBITIONS AND MUSEUMS

Experiential licensing includes interactive exhibitions and museums that offer fans the opportunity to explore the character's universe through exhibits, hands-on activities, and multimedia presentations.

Example: The Marvel Avengers S.T.A.T.I.O.N. (Scientific Training and Tactical Intelligence Operative Network) is an interactive exhibition located in various cities worldwide. Visitors can engage in immersive experiences, such as testing their strength against the Hulk or exploring Iron Man's suit, as they learn about the characters and their powers.

THEMED EVENTS AND FAN CONVENTIONS

Experiential licensing extends to themed events and fan conventions, where fans can gather to celebrate their favorite characters. These events often feature cosplay contests, panel discussions, interactive exhibits, and opportunities to meet actors and creators associated with the characters.

Example: San Diego Comic-Con International is one of the most prominent fan conventions where character licensing takes center stage. Attendees can participate in panel discussions with industry professionals, explore exhibitor booths showcasing licensed merchandise, and immerse themselves in the vibrant cosplay culture, bringing characters to life (Comic-Con International, n.d.).

Experiential licensing offers fans the opportunity to engage with characters in immersive and interactive ways, creating memorable and transformative experiences. By expanding beyond traditional merchandise, character entertainment licensors and licensees can tap into fans' desires for deeper connections with their favorite characters and build long-lasting brand loyalty.

THE ROLE OF INTELLECTUAL PROPERTY RIGHTS

Intellectual property rights, such as trademarks and copyrights, are critical considerations in Character Entertainment Licensing. Licensors need to ensure that their intellectual property rights are protected, while licensees need to obtain the necessary permissions and licenses to use the character's intellectual property in their products and experiences.

By understanding these and other key considerations in Character Entertainment Licensing, businesses and entrepreneurs can better navigate the industry and take advantage of the many opportunities it offers.

Intellectual property rights play a vital role in Character Entertainment Licensing, ensuring the protection of the characters and their associated elements. Here are key aspects and examples related to intellectual property rights in this context:

TRADEMARKS:

Trademarks safeguard the brand names, logos, symbols, and other distinctive elements associated with characters. Licensors must protect their trademarks to maintain exclusive rights to use them.

Example: The Walt Disney Company holds trademarks for characters like Mickey Mouse, ensuring that only authorized licensees can use the character's name and image on products.

COPYRIGHTS:

Copyrights protect original creative works, including character designs, storylines, illustrations, and audiovisual content. Licensors must secure copyrights to prevent unauthorized copying or distribution.

Example: DC Comics holds copyrights for Batman, granting them the exclusive right to reproduce and distribute comic books featuring the character.

LICENSING AGREEMENTS:

Licensees seeking to use characters in their products or experiences must obtain proper permissions through licensing agreements. These agreements outline the terms, conditions, and limitations for using the character's intellectual property.

Example: A video game developer enters into a licensing agreement with a character's rights holder to obtain the necessary rights to develop and release a video game based on the character.

ROYALTIES AND ROYALTY PAYMENTS:

Licensing agreements often involve royalty payments, where licensees pay a percentage of their sales or revenue to the licensors as compensation for using the character's intellectual property.

Example: A toy company that produces merchandise featuring a licensed character pays royalties to the character's rights holder based on the sales of those products.

BRAND PROTECTION AND ENFORCEMENT:

Licensors actively protect their intellectual property rights by monitoring the market for unauthorized use or infringement. They may take legal action against infringers to enforce their rights and maintain the integrity of the character.

Example: Marvel, as the licensor of characters like Iron Man, actively monitors the market for unauthorized merchandise featuring their characters and takes legal action against counterfeiters to protect their brand and intellectual property.

INTERNATIONAL CONSIDERATIONS:

Intellectual property rights can vary across different jurisdictions, requiring licensors and licensees to navigate international laws and regulations when licensing characters for global markets.

Example: When licensing a character for merchandise distribution in multiple countries, licensors must ensure they have the necessary intellectual property protections in each jurisdiction to maintain control over the character's use.

By understanding the importance of intellectual property rights and properly managing them through licensing agreements and legal protections, both licensors and licensees can ensure the authorized and profitable use of characters in commercial ventures.

The cost of developing a character entertainment property can vary greatly depending on several factors, including.

the type of property being developed, the complexity of the character's design and backstory, the level of talent and expertise involved in the development process, and the intended scope and scale of the property.

Here are some of the key cost factors to consider when developing a character entertainment property:

CONCEPT AND DESIGN

The first step in developing a character entertainment property is to conceptualize and design the character. This can involve creating sketches, digital renderings, and/or 3D models of the character, as well as defining its personality, backstory, and other key attributes.

The cost of this stage will depend on the level of detail and complexity involved in the character's design, as well as the talent and expertise of the concept artists and designers involved. For a simple character design, this stage could cost anywhere from a few hundred to a few thousand dollars. For a more complex character design, the cost could range from several thousand to tens of thousands of dollars. Concept and Design in Character Entertainment Licensing

Concept and design are crucial aspects of developing a character entertainment property. Here is an overview of the process and examples related to concept and design:

CHARACTER CREATION:

The initial step involves creating the character's concept, which includes its visual appearance, personality, traits, and background story. This phase requires brainstorming and ideation to develop a character that is unique, appealing, and suitable for various media and consumer products.

Example: Pixar's character design process involves extensive research, sketches, and iterations to create memorable characters like Woody from "Toy Story" or Wall-E from the movie of the same name.

VISUAL DESIGN:

Visual design encompasses the artistic representation of the character. It involves creating detailed sketches, illustrations, or digital renderings that bring the character to life visually. This stage focuses on refining the character's appearance, including its facial features, body shape, clothing, accessories, and color palette.

Example: The visual design process for Sonic the Hedgehog involved iterations and feedback from fans and consumers to ensure the character's design aligned with their expectations.

3D MODELING:

In many cases, characters are developed using 3D modeling software to create three-dimensional representations. This allows for more realistic and versatile character assets that can be used in various media, such as video games, animation, and merchandise.

Example: The character Groot from Marvel's "Guardians of the Galaxy" was designed using 3D modeling techniques to create a lifelike and expressive character for both movies and merchandise.

PERSONALITY AND BACKSTORY:

Giving the character a distinct personality and backstory helps to establish a deeper connection with the audience. This involves defining the character's motivations, relationships, strengths, weaknesses, and any relevant story arcs.

Example: The character Elsa from Disney's "Frozen" was developed with a complex personality, reflecting her struggle with self-acceptance and her journey of empowerment, which resonated strongly with audiences.

ITERATIVE PROCESS:

Concept and design are typically iterative processes, involving feedback, revisions, and refinements to achieve the desired character. Collaboration between artists, writers, and creative teams helps to shape and enhance the character's overall appeal and marketability.

Example: The design of the character Iron Man underwent multiple iterations and enhancements in the Marvel comics and movies, continuously adapting to the changing preferences and expectations of the audience.

BRAND CONSISTENCY:

During the concept and design phase, it is essential to ensure that the character's visual elements and personality align with the overall brand and narrative. This consistency helps to build a recognizable and cohesive brand identity.

Example: The character Mickey Mouse has maintained a consistent design and personality throughout its history, contributing to the character's enduring popularity and brand recognition.

By investing time and effort into concept and design, char-acter entertainment licensors and creators can develop compelling and iconic characters that resonate with audiences across different media and consumer products.

INTELLECTUAL PROPERTY PROTECTION

Once the character design is finalized, it's important to protect the character's intellectual property rights through trademark and/or copyright registration. The cost of these registrations can vary depending on the type of protection sought, as well as the legal fees involved. Generally, trademark registration costs range from a few hundred to a few thousand dollars, while copyright registration costs are typically in the range of several hundred dollars.

After finalizing the character design, it is crucial to protect the character's intellectual property rights through various legal mechanisms. Here is an overview of the intellectual property protection options and examples:

TRADEMARK REGISTRATION:

Trademarks protect the distinctive elements that identify and distinguish a character or brand from others in the marketplace. This can include the character's name, logo, or specific visual features associated with the character.

Example: The Walt Disney Company holds numerous trade-mark registrations for its characters, such as Mickey Mouse, including their names, logos, and specific design elements.

COPYRIGHT REGISTRATION:

Copyright protects original creative works, including visual arts, illustrations, sculptures, and written materials. In the context of character entertainment licensing, copyright protects the character design, illustrations, storylines, and other related works.

Example: Warner Bros. holds copyright registrations for the character Batman, which cover various aspects like the character's visual representation, comic books, films, and related merchandise.

LICENSING AGREEMENTS:

Licensing agreements serve as legal contracts between the character owner (licensor) and the party using the character (licensee). These agreements outline the terms and conditions for the authorized use of the character's intellectual property, including the scope, duration, territories, and royalty or licensing fees.

Example: Marvel Studios, a subsidiary of The Wal Disney Company, licenses its characters to video game companies, such as Sony Interactive Entertainment, for the development and distribution of games based on characters like Spider-Man.

ENFORCEMENT AND LITIGATION:

Intellectual property owners must actively enforce their rights to prevent unauthorized use or infringement of their characters. This may involve monitoring the market for un-authorized products, issuing cease and desist letters, and pursuing legal action if necessary.

Example: The Pokémon Company actively protects its characters and trademarks by taking legal action against unauthorized use or infringement. This includes enforcing their rights against counterfeit merchandise or unauthorized fan creations.

INTERNATIONAL PROTECTION:

Intellectual property protection should be considered on an international level, especially if the character or brand has a global presence or potential for expansion. This may involve filing for trademarks and copyrights in multiple jurisdictions to ensure comprehensive protection.

Example: The character Hello Kitty, owned by Sanrio, has global recognition, and is protected by intellectual property rights in various countries to safeguard its brand and character integrity.

Securing intellectual property rights is crucial for businesses that want to maintain their competitive edge and prevent others from profiting off their ideas or creations. It also allows for licensing opportunities and can increase the overall value of a company. Intellectual property protection for character entertainment properties is essential to safeguard the rights of licensors and prevent unauthorized use by others. By obtaining trademark and copyright registrations and establishing proper licensing agreements, character owners can effectively protect their creations and maintain control over their characters' commercial use.

CONTENT DEVELOPMENT

Once the character is designed and protected, the next step is to develop content around the character, such as stories, artwork, and animations. The cost of this stage will depend on the scope and scale of the content being developed, as well as the talent and expertise involved in the development process.

For example, a simple comic book or short animation could cost anywhere from a few thousand to tens of thousands of dollars to produce, while a feature-length film or video game could cost millions of dollars or more to develop.

CONTENT DEVELOPMENT IN CHARACTER ENTERTAINMENT LICENSING

After designing and protecting a character, the next crucial step is to develop compelling content that showcases the character's stories, artwork, and animations. Here are some key considerations and detailed examples for con-tent development in character entertainment licensing:

STORYTELLING AND NARRATIVE DEVELOPMENT:

Creating engaging and captivating stories around the character is essential for connecting with the audience and building a loyal fan base.

Example: The Harry Potter franchise, created by J.K. Rowling, features a rich narrative that spans seven books, which were later adapted into successful film adaptations. The captivating storylines and well-developed characters contributed to its immense popularity and success.

COMICS AND GRAPHIC NOVELS:

Comics and graphic novels provide an excellent medium for showcasing the character's adventures and expanding the character's universe.

Example: The Marvel Comics universe features a vast array of characters, such as Spider-Man, Iron Man, and the Avengers. These characters have been showcased in nu-merous comic book series, enabling fans to delve deeper into their stories and follow their ongoing adventures.

ANIMATED TV SHOWS AND FILMS:

Developing animated TV shows and films allows the char-acter to come to life and engage with the audience visually and through storytelling.

Example: The character SpongeBob SquarePants was ini-tially introduced through an animated TV series that has garnered a massive fan base. The show's success has led to the development of several films, expanding the character's presence and reaching wider audiences.

DIGITAL CONTENT AND WEBISODES:

Creating digital content, such as webisodes or short ani-mated clips, provides an opportunity to engage with audiences on digital platforms and social media.

Example: The Angry Birds franchise initially gained popularity through its mobile game, and later expanded into animated webisodes and digital content. These bite-sized episodes helped keep fans engaged and further promoted the brand and its characters.

ARTWORK AND ILLUSTRATIONS:

Developing artwork and illustrations showcasing the character in various poses, expressions, and settings is crucial for merchandise and promotional materials.

Example: The character Hello Kitty, created by Sanrio, is known for its cute and iconic artwork. The character's de-sign is featured on various products, including clothing, stationary, and accessories, making it highly recognizable and sought after by fans worldwide.

INTERACTIVE MEDIA AND GAMING:

Creating interactive media, such as video games or mobile apps, offers a unique way for fans to immerse themselves in the character's world and actively participate in their adventures.

Example: The Pokémon franchise has expanded into various video games, allowing players to catch, train, and battle with Pokémon characters. These games provide an interactive experience that appeals to fans of all ages.

Content development plays a crucial role in character entertainment licensing as it brings the character to life, captivates the audience, and drives engagement and merchandise sales. By creating compelling stories, leveraging different media platforms, and producing high-quality artwork and animations, character owners can establish a strong connection with fans and ensure the longevity and success of their character in the entertainment industry.

MARKETING AND PROMOTION

Once the content is developed, it's important to market and promote the character entertainment property to potential licensees, partners, and consumers. The cost of marketing and promotion can vary depending on the channels used and the scale of the campaign but can range from a few thousand to several hundred thousand dollars or more.

MARKETING AND PROMOTION IN CHARACTER ENTERTAINMENT LICENSING

Once the content for a character entertainment property is developed, it's crucial to effectively market and promote the property to reach potential licensees, partners, and consumers. Here are some key considerations and de-tailed examples for marketing and promotion in character entertainment licensing:

BRANDING AND IDENTITY:

Establish a strong and consistent brand identity for the character and the property, including logos, taglines, and visual elements that reflect the character's essence.

Example: The Disney brand is known for its iconic logo and tagline, "The Happiest Place on Earth." This branding consistently represents the magical and family-friendly experience associated with Disney characters and properties.

TRADITIONAL ADVERTISING:

Utilize traditional advertising channels, such as television commercials, print media, billboards, and radio spots, to reach a wide audience.

Example: When promoting a new movie featuring a popular character, studios often invest in television advertisements, billboards in high-traffic areas, and magazine spreads to generate buzz and attract audiences.

DIGITAL MARKETING:

Leverage digital platforms and online marketing strategies to reach target audiences, engage fans, and create a digital presence for the character and property.

Example: Social media platforms like Instagram, Facebook, and Twitter are commonly used to share character updates, behind-the-scenes content, and interact with fans directly. Paid online advertising, influencer collaborations, and search engine optimization can also boost visibility.

LICENSING EXPOS AND TRADE SHOWS:

Participate in industry-specific expos and trade shows to showcase the character and attract potential licensees, partners, and retailers.

Example: Licensing Expo, held annually in Las Vegas, brings together licensors, licensees, retailers, and industry professionals to showcase and negotiate licensing deals. Exhibiting at such events allows character owners to net-work and connect with key industry players.

CROSS-PROMOTIONS AND COLLABORATIONS:

Collaborate with other brands or properties that align with the character's values and target audience to expand reach and attract new fans.

Example: McDonald's often collaborates with popular characters, such as those from movies or animated series, to create themed Happy Meal toys or promotional tie-ins. This cross-promotion benefits both the fast-food chain and the character's franchise by increasing exposure and generating consumer interest.

MERCHANDISING AND PRODUCT PLACEMENT:

Develop a wide range of merchandise featuring the char-acter, including toys, clothing, accessories, and collectibles. Additionally, explore product placement opportunities in films, TV shows, and other media.

Example: The Star Wars franchise has an extensive line of merchandise, including action figures, apparel, and home decor. The strategic placement of Star Wars products with-in the franchise's movies and TV shows further enhances brand recognition and drives sales.

PUBLICITY AND EVENTS:

Generate publicity through press releases, media inter-views, and special events centered around the character, such as character meet-and-greets, conventions, or themed activations.

Example: Comic-Con International, held annually in San Diego, attracts a vast audience of fans and industry pro-fessionals. Major studios and fran-chises often leverage this event to announce new projects, showcase exclu-sive content, and interact with fans directly.

The cost of marketing and promotion can vary significantly depending on factors such as the chosen channels, the scale of the campaign, and the target market. Marketing budgets can range from a few thousand dollars for smaller campaigns to several hundred thousand dollars or more for larger-scale initiatives. It's important to allocate resources effectively and tailor marketing strategies to reach the intended audience and maximize the property's exposure.

Successful marketing and promotion efforts are crucial in character enter-tainment licensing as they create awareness, generate interest, and drive consumer engagement and sales. By employing a mix of traditional adver-tising, digital marketing, cross-promotions, and publicity events, character owners can increase Licensing and Merchandising.

Finally, the cost of licensing and merchandising the character entertainment property will depend on the type and number of license agreements entered, as well as the level of oversight and control required to maintain brand consistency and quality.

For example, a licensing agreement with a toy manufacturer could involve up-front costs for tooling and production, as well as ongoing royalty fees based on sales. The cost of these fees will depend on the terms of the agreement and the volume of sales generated.

Overall, the cost of developing a character entertainment property can range from a few thousand dollars to tens of millions of dollars, depending on the scope and scale of the property being developed. It's important to carefully consider all the cost factors involved, as well as the potential return on investment, before embarking on a character entertainment property development project.

LEGAL AND REGULATORY COMPLIANCE

Another important cost factor to consider when developing a character entertainment property is legal and regulatory compliance. This can include compliance with industry-specific regulations, such as those related to children's content, as well as compliance with broader legal requirements related to data privacy, intellectual property rights, and consumer protection.

The cost of legal and regulatory compliance will depend on the complexity of the regulations involved, as well as the legal and compliance expertise required to ensure compliance. For example, compliance with children's content regulations could involve additional costs for content moderation and age verification measures, while compliance with data privacy regulations could require investment in data security and compliance auditing.

LEGAL AND REGULATORY COMPLIANCE IN CHARACTER ENTERTAINMENT LICENSING

When developing a character entertainment property, it is crucial to ensure legal and regulatory compliance. This includes complying with industry-specific regulations and broader legal requirements. Here are some key considerations and detailed examples for legal and regulatory compliance in character entertainment licensing:

INDUSTRY-SPECIFIC REGULATIONS:

Children's Content Regulations: If the character entertainment property targets children as its primary audience, it is essential to comply with regulations regarding content appropriateness, age ratings, and advertising restrictions.

Example: The Children's Online Privacy Protection Act (COPPA) in the United States imposes strict rules on the collection of personal information from children under the age of 13. Compliance with COPPA ensures the protection of children's privacy rights.

INTELLECTUAL PROPERTY RIGHTS:

Trademark Protection: Register trademarks associated with the character's name, logo, or distinctive elements to establish legal ownership and prevent unauthorized use.

Example: The Walt Disney Company has registered trademarks for its popular characters, such as Mickey Mouse and Cinderella, to protect their brand identity and prevent infringement.

COPYRIGHT PROTECTION:

Ensure that the content developed for the character, such as stories, artwork, and animations, is protected by copyright. This grants exclusive rights to reproduce, distribute, and display the copyrighted material.

Example: Marvel Comics holds copyrights for its iconic superhero characters, including Spider-Man and Iron Man, protecting their stories and visual representations.

DATA PRIVACY AND SECURITY:

Compliance with Data Protection Laws: If the character entertainment property collects personal information from users or engages in online activities, such as mobile apps or websites, compliance with data protection laws is essential.

Example: The General Data Protection Regulation (GDPR) in the European Union sets strict guidelines for the collection, processing, and storage of personal data. ("SaaS and Data Privacy: Regulatory Compliance and Investor Concerns") Adhering to GDPR ensures the protection of user data and privacy rights.

CONSUMER PROTECTION:

Advertising Standards: Adhere to advertising standards and guidelines to ensure that promotional materials for the character entertainment property are accurate, truthful, and do not mislead consumers.

Example: The Federal Trade Commission (FTC) in the United States monitors and enforces advertising standards to protect consumers from deceptive or unfair practices.

PRODUCT SAFETY REGULATIONS:

If the character entertainment property includes physical products, such as toys or merchandise, compliance with product safety regulations is crucial to ensure that the products meet safety standards.

Example: The Consumer Product Safety Commission (CPSC) in the United States sets safety requirements for toys, ensuring that they are free from hazards and pose no risks to children.

It is important to consult legal experts or intellectual property professionals who specialize in entertainment and licensing to ensure compliance with all relevant laws and regulations. Failing to comply can result in legal disputes, reputational damage, and financial penalties. ("Project-Based Staffing in UK – Staffing Agency UK")

Legal and regulatory compliance is a critical aspect of character entertainment licensing, as it protects the rights of the character's owners, ensures consumer safety, and maintains the integrity of the property. By understanding and fulfilling legal obligations, character owners can establish a solid foundation for their licensing ventures.

TALENT AND EXPERTISE

The development of a character entertainment property often requires the involvement of a range of talented and experienced professionals, including concept artists, writers, animators, voice actors, and producers. The cost of these professionals will depend on their level of experience and expertise, as well as the scope and scale of the project.

For example, the cost of hiring a seasoned animation director or voice actor could be significantly higher than the cost of hiring a less experienced professional. Additionally, the cost of talent and expertise can increase if the development process involves international collaboration or cross-disciplinary collaboration Talent and Expertise in Character Entertainment Licensing.

The development of a character entertainment property relies on the contributions of various talented and experienced professionals. These individuals play vital roles in bringing the character to life and creating engaging content. Here are some key roles and examples of professionals involved in character entertainment licensing:

CONCEPT ARTISTS:

Concept artists are responsible for visualizing and designing the appearance and attributes of the character. They create sketches, digital renderings, or 3D models that serve as the foundation for the character's visual representation.

Example: In the creation of iconic characters like Mickey Mouse or Pikachu, concept artists, such as Ubiwerks and Ken Sugimori respectively, contributed their artistic skills to develop the distinctive and recognizable features of these beloved characters.

WRITERS:

Writers play a crucial role in shaping the character's per-sonality, backstory, and the narratives in which they are involved. They create engaging stories and dialogues that captivate audiences and enhance the character's overall appeal.

Example: J.K. Rowling, the author of the Harry Potter series, developed the rich and immersive world of Harry Potter, including the character's background, relationships, and adventures, which became the foundation for successful character licensing across various mediums.

ANIMATOR

Animators bring characters to life through movement and expression. They create animations, whether in traditional hand-drawn or digital formats, that showcase the character's personality, actions, and emotions.

Example: The team of animators at Pixar Animation Studios played a pivotal role in developing beloved characters like Woody and Buzz Lightyear from the Toy Story franchise. Their expertise in animation brought these characters to life and contributed to their popularity and merchandising success.

VOICE ACTORS:

Voice actors provide the character's voice, infusing it with personality, emotion, and distinct vocal traits. They give the character a unique voice that resonates with audiences and adds depth to their portrayal.

Example: James Earl Jones, known for his deep and commanding voice, provided the iconic voice of Darth Vader in the Star Wars franchise. His powerful performance contributed to the character's impact and recognition, making Darth Vader one of the most popular characters in licensing history.

PRODUCERS:

Producers oversee the overall development and production process of the character entertainment property. They coordinate the efforts of various teams and ensure that the vision for the character is realized across different mediums and licensing opportunities.

Example: Kevin Feige, the president of Marvel Studios, has been instrumental in overseeing the Marvel Cinematic Universe. His role as a producer has involved coordinating the development of characters like Iron

Man, Captain America, and Black Widow, leading to successful character licensing across films, merchandise, and more.

These professionals, among others, collaborate to create cohesive and compelling character entertainment properties. Their talent and expertise contribute to the success and longevity of characters in licensing, allowing them to resonate with audiences and become valuable intellectual properties.

It is essential for character owners and licensors to assemble a team of skilled professionals who understand the character's essence and can effectively bring it to life.

Collaborating with experienced individuals across various disciplines ensures the quality and marketability of the character entertainment property.

TECHNOLOGY AND INFRASTRUCTURE

The use of technology and infrastructure is also an important cost consideration when developing a character entertainment property. This can include the cost of software and hardware used for content creation and production, as well as the cost of hosting and delivering digital content.

The cost of technology and infrastructure will depend on the scale and complexity of the project, as well as the technological requirements involved. For example, the cost of developing a virtual reality experience based on the character's brand could involve significant investment in specialized hardware and software, as well as in content creation and production.

TECHNOLOGY AND INFRASTRUCTURE IN CHARACTER ENTERTAINMENT LICENSING

The development of a character entertainment property often relies on technology and infrastructure to facilitate content creation, production, and distribution. Here are some key aspects of technology and infrastructure that are important considerations in character entertainment licensing, along with detailed examples:

CONTENT CREATION SOFTWARE AND HARDWARE:

The cost of software and hardware used for content creation is a significant consideration. Depending on the complexity and requirements of the character entertainment property, various tools may be needed, such as graphic design software, animation software, and audio editing software.

Example: Adobe Creative Cloud suite is commonly used by professionals in character entertainment licensing.

Software applications like Adobe Photoshop, Illustrator, and After Effects are utilized for character design, artwork, animation, and post-production processes.

ANIMATION AND RENDERING TOOLS:

For animated character properties, specialized animation and rendering tools are necessary to bring characters to life and create visually appealing content.

Example: Autodesk Maya and Pixar's Render Man are widely used in the animation industry. Maya offers a comprehensive set of tools for 3D modeling, rigging, and animation, while Render Man provides advanced rendering capabilities to achieve high-quality visuals.

DIGITAL ASSET MANAGEMENT SYSTEMS:

Managing and organizing digital assets, such as character designs, artwork, and animation files, is crucial for efficient collaboration and future use. Digital asset management systems help streamline the storage, retrieval, and distribution of these assets.

Example: By implementing digital asset management platforms like Widen or Bynder, character licensors and licensees can effectively organize and share digital assets, ensuring accessibility and consistency across different teams and projects.

CLOUD STORAGE AND HOSTING:

Storing and hosting digital content, including artwork, animations, and multimedia files, requires reliable and scalable cloud storage and hosting solutions. This enables easy access, backup, and distribution of content.

Example: Amazon Web Services (AWS) and Microsoft Azure are popular cloud service providers that offer scalable stor-age and hosting solutions. These platforms allow businesses to securely store and deliver digital content to end-users across various platforms.

CONTENT DELIVERY NETWORKS (CDNS):

CDNs are used to distribute digital content efficiently by delivering it from geographically distributed servers closer to end-users. This helps reduce latency and ensure smooth content streaming or downloading.

Example: Akamai Technologies and Cloudflare are well-known CDNs that assist in delivering digital content, including video, images, and interactive experiences, to global audiences with improved performance and reliability.

E-COMMERCE PLATFORMS:

For selling licensed merchandise and products, having an e-commerce platform is essential. These platforms provide the infrastructure for online sales, inventory management, payment processing, and order fulfillment.

Example: Shopify and WooCommerce are popular e-commerce platforms that offer customizable online stores, integration with payment gateways, and inventory management features for character licensors and licensees to sell their products directly to consumers.

These examples highlight the importance of leveraging technology and infrastructure to streamline content creation, production, and distribution processes in character entertainment licensing. By investing in the right tools and systems, li-censors and licensees can enhance efficiency, reduce costs, and ensure a seamless user experience for their target audience.

In conclusion, the development of a character entertainment property involves numerous factors that contribute to the overall cost and success of the venture. Throughout this book, we have explored various aspects of character entertainment licensing and the associated costs, providing detailed examples and insights. Here is a summary of the key points discussed:

Concept and Design: The initial conceptualization and de-sign of a character lay the foundation for its appeal and marketability. The cost varies based on factors such as artistic talent, complexity of design, and back-story development.

Intellectual Property Protection: Protecting the character's intellectual property rights through trademark and copy-right registration is crucial to ensure exclusive rights and prevent unauthorized use.

Content Development: Creating engaging and captivating content, including stories, artwork, and animations, is essential to attracting and retaining audiences. Costs can vary depending on the scope, quality, and talent involved in content creation.

Marketing and Promotion: Effective marketing and pro-motion strategies are necessary to create awareness and generate interest in the character entertainment property. Costs can range from modest campaigns to large-scale, multi-channel marketing efforts.

Licensing and Merchandising: Licensing the character for merchandise and other commercial opportunities can pro-vide additional revenue streams. Costs may include licensing fees, product development, manufacturing, and distribution.

Legal and Regulatory Compliance: Complying with industry – specific regulations and broader legal requirements re-lated to intellectual property, data privacy, and consumer protection is essential to avoid legal issues and protect the brand's integrity.

Talent and Expertise: Collaborating with skilled professionals, such as concept artists, writers, animators, voice actors, and producers, is crucial for the successful development and execution of a character entertainment property.

Technology and Infrastructure: Leveraging technology and infrastructure, including content creation tools, digital asset management systems, cloud storage, and e-commerce platforms, helps streamline processes and enhance efficiency.

Character entertainment property development costs can fluctuate widely depending on these elements, as well as the project's specific objectives, scope, and intended audience. To get the best results, you need to put in the time and effort into planning, making strategic decisions, and allocating resources wisely

GLOSSARY

Character Entertainment Licensing: The process of granting permission to use and/or reproduce a character for commercial purposes.

Intellectual Property: Intangible creations of the mind, such as characters, artwork, and stories, that are protected by law. It includes trademarks, copyrights, and patents.

Brand Recognition: The level of awareness and familiarity that consumers have with a particular brand or character.

Fan Base: The dedicated group of individuals who are passionate about a specific character, franchise, or intellectual property.

Content Development: The creation of stories, artwork, animations, and other media related to a character or franchise.

Licensing Agreement: A legal contract that grants permission to a licensee to use a character's intellectual property in specified ways, typically in exchange for financial compensation.

Merchandising: The production and sale of licensed merchandise, such as toys, clothing, accessories, and collectibles, featuring a character or franchise.

Trademark: A distinctive symbol, word, phrase, or logo used to identify and distinguish the goods or services of one entity from those of others.

Copyright: The exclusive legal right granted to the creator of an original work, such as a story or artwork, to reproduce, distribute, and display the work.

Royalties: Financial compensation paid by a licensee to the licensor based on a percentage of sales or revenue generated from the licensed products or experiences.

Licensing Fee: The upfront payment made by a licensee to the licensor for the right to use the character's intellectual property.

Concept Art: Visual representations, such as sketches or digital renderings, that depict the initial design and visual style of a character.

Brand Identity: The unique combination of visual elements, messaging, and values that define a character or brand.

Marketing Campaign: A coordinated series of promotional activities designed to raise awareness, generate interest, and drive sales of licensed products and experiences.

Target Audience: The specific group of consumers for whom a character or licensed products are primarily intended.

Digital Asset Management: A system or process for organizing, storing, and distributing digital assets, such as artwork, animations, and promotional materials, industry standards, and ethical guidelines.

Compliance: Adherence to legal and regulatory requirements

E-commerce: The buying and selling of goods and services over the internet.

Content Delivery Network (CDN): A geographically distributed network of servers that deliver digital content to end-users more efficiently and reliably.

Data Privacy: The protection and proper handling of personal information collected from users or customers in accordance with applicable privacy laws and regulations.

Product Safety Regulations: Standards and requirements established to ensure that products, such as toys and merchandise, meet safety guidelines and do not pose risks to consumers.